Acknowledgement

I would like to thank my parents for making me who I am today, my friends who have always supported me. Many thanks to my college who provided me with the platform to learn and grow myself as an individual. Finally I would like to thank my readers to take out the time and read this book. I hope you get useful information out of it.

Preface

We live in a world where almost every aspect of our life is controlled in some way or the other by technology. Whether we like it or not, we are so much dependent on technology that we cannot imagine to live without it. Though it has definitely made our lives easier, such dependency has some serious repercussions. Security has become so much prominent that companies spend insane amount of money to protect its data from hackers. One might think that on a personal level, it is not that important to care about these things, however nothing can be fu-rther from the truth. "Ignorance is bliss" is probably just the opposite of what I am trying to convey here. Because this world of internet is huge and you will find every type of person here- one who likes you, one who hates you, one who want to steal every single penny of yours. I'll give you numerous examples where people got scammed of their hard-earned money so I cannot stress enough on how important this awareness is. It is important that we take care of ourselves.

This book will show you exactly how hackers try to attack people (not physically) and how you can defend yourself against them. Most articles or well-wishers suggest you to follow some things without actually explaining why it is that way and most of the time it becomes over defensive. Just keeping a complex password using unthinkable characters and numbers won't save you from hackers. It is definitely possible to survive without an antivirus if you know what you are doing. But you have to be aware of why you are doing things a certain way and why that is necessary. Only then you can consider yourself shielded enough against the bad elements of this world.

About me

Before starting, it is important that you know about me and where all this holy knowledge comes from, not only because you can catch and blame me if your account gets hacked in future, but also because I want to establish a trust between us.

I have done my B.E. from Delhi College of Engineering (now DTU) in the year 2012 (if that matters). I am not a security or networking expert by profession, but I think of myself to be more than qualified to educate anyone regarding online security. By profession I am a software engineer and an ethical hacker by hobby. Please don't curse me for that; fortunately hacker is a misnomer and a hacker is not the bad guy who wants to steal your information. It is a term which got infamous over time. However I will continue to use the term hacker the way you think it is to avoid confusion. Personally, I have been to the dark side of hacking without crossing the lines of morality and legality, so I know exactly how hackers operate and what they do to achieve their goals. This inside information is very helpful for staying protected in this online world of scam and fraud.

My aim in this book is to explain you how to stay safe from any kind of online scam or hacking attempt and to enable you to guard yourself from every possible kind of attack. I will try to do this without going into the technical details, however there are tips in between for the tech-savvy. Whenever you see the "Pro Tip" title, and you do not understand the content, do not worry because it is not intended for you and it is no way a requirement to understand the concept. Overall, I really believe that you will benefit with this information whether you are just a normal computer user, a student or a technically sound professional.

Table of Contents

Who should read this book?

This book is for everyone except those who think they can never be hacked or scammed. You'd be surprised that how many people think they are smart enough but they are the first ones to get into a trap. I have seen the most tech savvy of people being ignorant about basic security norms. Even if you are a hacker yourself, I am sure you will enjoy reading this book and maybe learn a few things. This is my first book so I really hope that I do it the right way by keeping it interesting as well as informative.

Please note that I will try to use very simple language without dwelling into technical details so that a common person without any internal know-how should be able understand it. If something is extremely obvious for you, please don't feel offended.

One more thing I would like to emphasize here is that I started this book with the sole motto of spreading awareness (along with some part time income along the way if it allows). I would like you to do the same by sharing this knowledge with your friends and family and preventing them from getting scammed in future. As much as I would like you to recommend this book to others, I would be more than happy if you lend it to as many people you can. Because that's what we do – protect those whom we love.

Who are hackers and what they want?

So, who the hell are these people, and what do they get by doing those nasty things? The motive behind every attack is different. First thing is to understand the target of the attack. A hacker's target can vary from a large or small company, governments, organizations, high net worth individuals or a common man. Every attack has a motive behind it. By attacking an organization, I mean taking control over the websites/server and disrupting the services which the organization provides. So, when a company gets attacked, you might not be able to access its website and the database where all the customer's information is stored can also be compromised.

The reason for attacking the organizations may be to send a message or to prove a point. Also, companies get attacked for sensitive data their computers contain which is generally of some monetary value. Some websites get attacked just because they happen to be in a specific country which the hacker doesn't like. The reason to hack a common person like you and me may be either to scam for money or to take revenge on someone.

But if you are reading this book, chances are that you don't have to worry about an organization or government getting hacked. So, why would a hacker be interested in you? Well, here are a few reasons:

- To scam you out of your money. This is the most common reason. People who want to make some quick bucks and do not care about morality or legality will play every kind of trick to fool you. I will explain how to identify such threats.

- It might a person you know who might try to hack your account, maybe to just have fun with you or to take revenge against you. In any case, you have to be very careful.

- To get your computer's resources. It might be surprising for you but a huge number of viruses and Trojans actually have a single motive to hack you i.e. to use your computer's resources to achieve their higher goal. For instance, to carry out an attack against an organization or government, a hacker needs CPU power. His own computer can give him a limited amount of CPU power. So he creates a virus which spreads in thousands of computer. When your computer is infected by such virus, your machine becomes a "slave" which gets involved in the attack by the hacker against his target organization. When thousands of slaves attack the target server, it becomes a powerful tool for the hacker. Also, the hacker hides behind your system and your IP address which makes it difficult for the police authorities to track him. The situation can be understood better by the following diagram. Zombies are the slave computers and the victim is target organization's server (although technically zombies can also be victim)

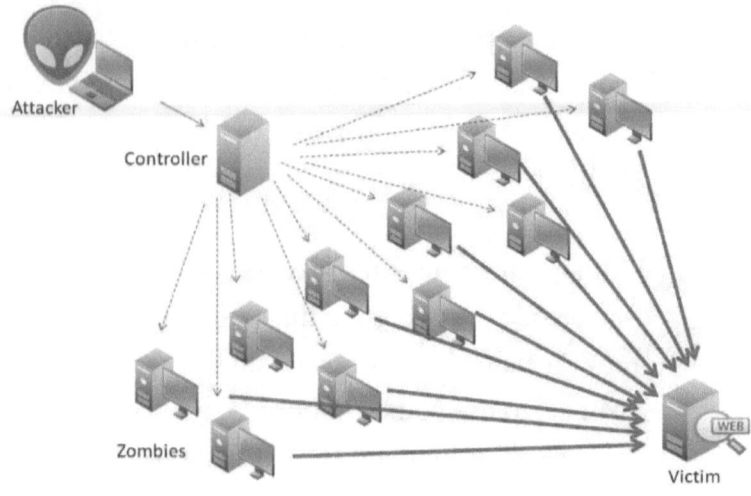

Some incidents to scare you

I am going to share with you real life incidents where people got ripped off; this can be a lesson for others to not repeat the mistake.

Crypto locker Virus

On September 2013, hackers unleashed this ransom virus on internet which encrypted the personal files of victims and asked $300 as payment to unlock the files. Those who did not pay were not able to get their files back and at that time, there was no way of removing the virus or getting the files restored without paying the money to hackers. Even now, if someone gets infected by the virus, it is not an easy task to recover the files. For the people who store sensitive and important documents on their computer, it becomes an absolute necessity to get their files back and sometimes there is no option but to actually pay the amount and hope that hackers remain true to their word by unlocking the files.

This is how it looks after your computer is infected:

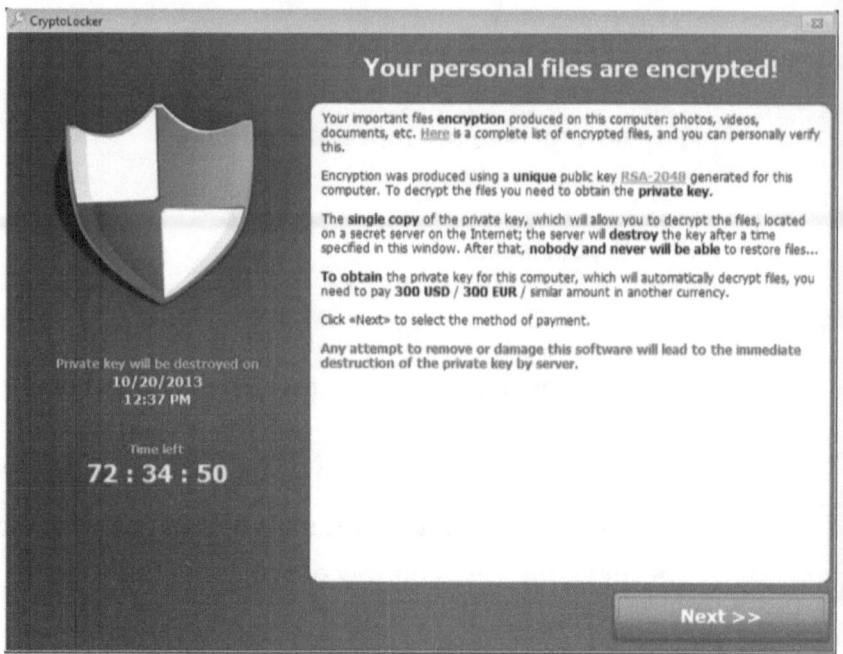

The hackers were able to successfully extort more than $3 million dollar from the victims around the world.

You may ask how people got infected. The victims got an email pretending to be from a legitimate company with an attachment (which had this virus hidden behind a pdf file). I will cover it later in detail about how these kind of viruses can enter your computer and how not to get trapped like this.

Nigerian mail scam

A person from New York when received the following e-mail thought he got the opportunity of a lifetime-
"DEAR SIR/MADAM: I REPRESENT THE RECENTLY DEPOSED MINISTER OF AGRICULTURE FOR NODAMBIZIA, WHO HAS EMBEZZLED 30 MILLION DOLLARS FROM HIS STARVING COUNTRYMEN AND NOW NEEDS TO GET IT OUT OF THE COUNTRY..."

The e-mail asks the victim to help the sender in getting millions of dollars getting out of country and in return they would share the profit. The complete e-mail was very long with a lot of convincing tactics. The person fell into the trap and deposited $5000 as costs of travel, bribery, administration etc. Later he was asked to come to Nigeria for physical meeting and when he got there he was threatened to deposit more money. The victim refused and the criminals killed him. There are thousands of such cases of which this is just a singled out example. The e-mail may or may not be convincing enough but thousands of people fall into these kind of traps which is getting this scam flourishing.

These are just a few examples. In reality, there are countless examples of people getting scammed for money. You can imagine that when a single type of virus can result in loss of $3 million dollar, how much amount all the viruses such scam schemes actually extort.

The angel savior

Sure, there are such bad people aiming to scam the crap out of you. But thankfully there is an angel savior to protect you. Would like to guess? If your guess is the cops or cyber-police, you are wrong. Those people have a lot more important things to do than finding out who hacked your Facebook account. Even if you suffered a monetary loss, there are so many scam cases every day that it is practically impossible for them to handle each of them. So unless, you lose a significant amount of money, you cannot rely or expect resolution by those agencies.

So who is it then? The only person who can save you is YOU. No really, I cannot stress enough on the fact that despite all the safety measures you take, despite all the strong security policies by Gmail and Facebook, there is always a weak link – you. You have to armor yourself and close this loop-hole. How exactly you ask? Well, to prevent yourself from getting hacked, you should – HACK. No, not exactly hack someone's account. It is:

H – Hard password

A – Antivirus update

C – Common sense

K – Keep your eyes open

Everyone tells you to do a hell lot of things to secure yourself online, and you can probably also find a book on 1001 ways to not get hacked. But accept it, we are humans and our memory is not that sharp to cram everything. Plus we have a lot more important things to remember. My way of teaching someone is to first demonstrate why and how things are done. Then it becomes so obvious and intuitive that you don't have to try to remember anything. In this book, I will demonstrate by examples, how you might fall into a trap and to prevent it. I will also give you a lot of tips which will be helpful in the long term. But all those tips and lessons can be broadly covered by this simple acronym – HACK. Believe me, there is nothing more you need to do than to remember this acronym. Any online threat can be circumvented by one of the above principles. I will not explain the acronym at this point. Rather, I will explain it one by one when needed in examples.

Getting hacked – Phishing

Suppose you have an account in a bank named *"Elite Bank"*. One fine day, you get an email from the bank:

From: no_reply@elitebank.com

Subject: Account Status

Dear Customer,

We recently noted some suspicious activity on your account. Someone tried to login into your account which did not look normal. For your security, we have temporarily prevented access to your account. Elite bank safeguards your account when there is a possibility that someone other than you tried to sign on. You may be getting this message because you signed in from a different location or device. If this is the case, your access may be restored when you return to your normal sign on method. The details of the device and location of the attempted login are as follows:

Time: *12:25:44, 04 Apr 2015*

Device: *Linux*

If it was you who was trying to access the account, there is no action needed from your side, however if the device or location does not look familiar to you, we recommend to IMMEDIATELY change your password. <u>Click here</u> to change your password and secure your account.

Regards

Joe Warne

Security Team

Elite Bank

You are instantly shocked to see this mail. You have not tried to recently login to the bank. Hell, you have never been to India in your life (as mentioned along the IP address). You are sure someone is trying to get into your account, so you instantly changed your password via the link provided in the mail.

A few days later, you notice some unauthorized/unrecognized transactions in your account accounting to large amount of money. Someone has used your account to purchase some online goods and/or transferred to some unknown bank account.

What went wrong?

What exactly happened there? You did your best to protect your account but in spite of that it got compromised. Let's revisit our case from the start. When you received the email about the unauthorized access, did you validate the sender of the email? How did you know that it was the bank itself sending the email? The e-mail could have come from anyone pretending to be from the bank.

So, if you did not even look at the 'From' field of the email, you failed at step 1. Now, if you are a cautious person and looked at the 'From' field of the email before believing or responding, it is a good practice. However, even then you are in a danger. Suppose the 'From' field is somewhat like this:

From: Security Team <**security@elitebank.com**>

The 'from' part of the email should end with the bank name or bank website. So in this case '@elitebank.com' looks trustworthy. If it was something else, like a public email provider – Gmail or yahoo etc., you should instantly know it is a scam. However please note that even if the email does end with the correct sender like in this case, you should not believe that it is the bank email even though it appears so. Reason – it is an easy task for the hacker to forge an e-mail, i.e. sending a spoofed email pretending to be coming from a source which is not the original one. The hacker doesn't even need to hack the bank website to achieve this. He can send email pretending to come from any email address- even your friends.

So, how do you find out whether this is the genuine sender? To be honest, for an average non-technical person, this is somewhat difficult. The best you can do is try to eliminate the obvious fake ones. For example, if the email is in capital letters, or has a lot of grammatical mistakes, most probably it is a scam. If an email passes all these filters and you are still in doubt, you should contact the person/bank directly through phone before responding to email.

<u>Pro Tip</u>

Using headers of an email, you can trace back the origin. Some online services are also there for this like the following: http://whatismyipaddress.com/trace-email

The next mistake you probably did here is to click the link in the mail (for password reset) without verifying its authenticity. True, we are somewhat casual while browsing online but if you are a sort of person who clicks the links blindly without even knowing where you are going, it needs to stop. You should NEVER click the links from unknown sources. Like for example in this e-mail, the password reset link actually takes you to a fake website which is a replica of your bank's website. When you try to reset your password, you end up giving up your existing credentials to the hacker. I will discuss this in detail later but for now understand that you have to careful while clicking links online.

What exactly is phishing?

Phishing is the most common way of getting your account compromised. Hackers who use phishing technique to scam are sometimes referred to as phishers. Using fake emails and crafty scams, phishers trawl the cyber high seas for your banking information, credit card numbers and passwords. Roughly 156 million phishing emails are sent globally every day, so even if a fraction fall for the scam, phishers score big. Here are some stats:

Number of phishing mails sent everyday:

156 million

Number of mails bypassing the spam filter:

16 million

Number of phishing mails opened by users:

8 million

Number of people falling into such trap everyday:
80,000

Phishing is basically a two-step process:

1. First, the hacker chooses a target method, say banking website. What the hacker would do is create a fake duplicate website of your bank which will look exactly similar to original. The only difference being that any information you give at the duplicate website goes to the hacker instead of your bank, including your bank password.

2. Second the important part is to lure the user to go to fake website instead of the original one. They do this by sending fake mails appearing to be originating from the bank asking you to click the link for any xyz reason. When you click that link, it takes you to the fake website and anything you type there, for example to login you would enter the username and password, all that information goes directly to the hacker. He can then later use your credentials to login into your bank and perform fraudulent transactions.

The second part is more difficult part for a hacker than the first one. You may wonder why you will just click on anything from inside an email. Sometimes, they disguise it so well that even the smartest fall for it. It all depends on creativity of the hacker and awareness of the user.

Let me give you another example of phishing – You have an account on Gmail and one day you get an email from Gmail's support team that your account is locked and you need to login again to enter some security questions etc. Firstly, any such email should be seen with suspicion. Remember out previous discussion regarding the authenticity of the sender. Now suppose you click the link from inside the email and are redirected to login to the Gmail page as below:

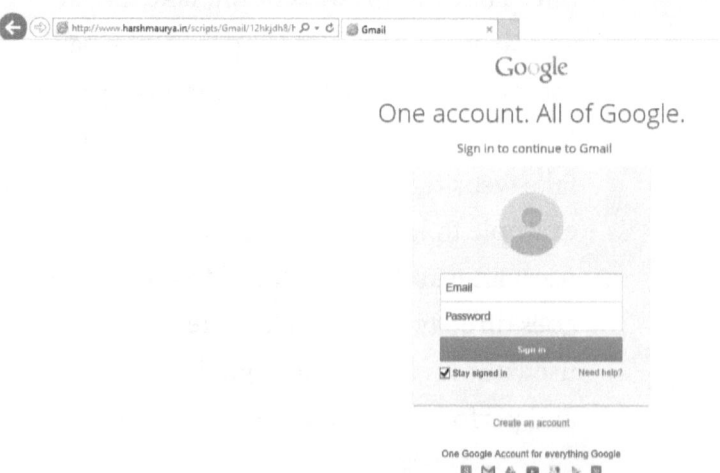

At the time of writing, this is very identical to the actual Gmail login page. How do you find out whether this is legitimate or a fake one? Well, one golden rule of thumb is to ALWAYS have a look at the URL address of the page you are visiting. So, if you look closely, the URL from the above image is something like:

If it was an original one, the URL would have been gmail.com or google.com or something similar, anything other than that is surely a fake one to trap you. Anything you type there is recorded and monitored by the hacker. In this case, I have created a fake phishing page on my personal website www.harshmaurya.in for demo purposes. If it was a real one by intended for malicious purpose, as soon as you enter your credentials, expecting to login, the username and password would be stored in some database owned by hacker and you will be sent back to Gmail so that you don't even realize that something wrong has happened. In this case, it does not matter how strong or complex your password is, because you are entering it all at a place where all of it is being recorded, so the advice you get from everyone to have a strong password is not sufficient to keep you safe. Another good practice to follow is to manually enter the website address in address bar of the browser rather than clicking links from anywhere, especially for banking websites. So if you want to go to your bank's website, rather than clicking link from any email, just enter it manually on the browser's address bar or if it is hard to remember, do a Google search for your bank's name and visit the website from there. In fact many banking websites have made it compulsory for user to manually enter the address in order to access the website. This is a good thing from a security point of view.

Now let us revisit our angel acronym- HACK and see how it can be used in safeguarding you against phishing. Using **C** for Common sense, we can straightaway infer that the email is a fake. Why would Gmail ask us to login again to review security settings? We are already logged in, remember? In the banking email, we could have used our common sense to either call the bank directly since it was an important issue or at least refrain from clicking links blindly. Using **K** for Keep your eyes open, any phishing attack can be averted. As already mentioned, always have a look at the URL of the page you are visiting and keep your eyes open to any suspicious thing you notice.

There can be many variations to the phishing attack and not just limited to banking or Gmail/yahoo related. In the end, it all comes down to the awareness of the user and how easily he/she can get trapped. Let's do a quick summary of what we learnt.

Summary

- ✓ Do not click links blindly while browsing online
- ✓ Any email can be forged easily. Always verify the authenticity of the sender
- ✓ Keep a look at the URL of the webpage you visit
- ✓ Use your common sense to filter out the obvious scam attempts.

Getting hacked – Malwares

Malwares are another class of hacking tools affecting millions of people worldwide. Malware is short for malicious software and is generic term used for all kinds of viruses, Trojans, Spyware, Adware etc. I will explain each of these terms shorty. A person from non-computer background might know only about the term virus since it is most widely used term by people. However, please note that it is done only for simplicity purpose as for a common person it is irrelevant what kind of malware his computer is infected with.

Many of you might have heard that computers are infected by virus and you yourself might have encountered them before. What do you do when your computer is infected by a virus? If you ask a tech savvy guy about it, he would probably run an antivirus scan on your machine and if the problem still persists, he would maybe recommend reformatting the whole system.

What makes computer viruses, Trojans and key loggers dangerous? Why should you care to remove them? Most importantly, how do they get inside your computer in the first place?

Before answering these questions, lets discuss about the repercussions of having a virus inside your computer and how can it affect you. I won't get into the technical details of differences between various class of malwares like virus, Trojan and key logger because it might not be relevant for all. I will however explain the basic difference between them and will use the generic term virus or malware to refer to these classes of infections.

What exactly is a computer virus?

It is an analogy from the real world, it represents an infection. For it to survive and sustain, it needs a host (your computer in this case). What do you do when your body is infected by a virus? The antibodies inside your body tries to fight against it and kill the infection. The medicines you take either boost your immune system or just help your body to recover, the medicines themselves doesn't fight the infection. Anyways, taking a break from the biology class, in computer world a virus is a computer program or software intended to do malicious things inside your computer. It is just a file however and just by looking at it, there is no way to tell whether the file is a virus or a genuine application. Below is a list of most common types of malwares and what trouble they can bring to your system:

1. **Virus:** Viruses are a nemesis for computer. They can do all kind of nasty things like deleting or corrupting important files, preventing you from doing normal computer operations, steal data, wasting computer resource, and spreading to other connected devices like a USB drive. The most distinguishing feature of virus is that it can spread to other systems by copying itself over. It can also hide itself very well so that you cannot delete a virus without the help of an anti-virus software.

2. **Key loggers** are program which record and monitor every keystroke you type via keyboard in your system and it send all this data to the hacker. So, every password you type in any website, your chat messages, your email communication all of that is revealed to the hacker and he can take control of all your online accounts. For this very reason, it is recommended to use **virtual keyboard** (or on screen keyboard) when typing a password. Because when by using a virtual keyboard, you are not physically pressing the keyboard buttons but instead using mouse to click the keyboard buttons on the computer screen which makes it difficult for the key logger to

monitor it if it is present on your system. Of course the ideal scenario would be that your system is free of any such key-logging malware but one can never be too careful.

3. **Trojans** are the deadliest ones which basically have the capability to own your computer. The hacker can do anything to your system as if he is physically present there. In addition to the functions of a key-logger, a Trojan can also use your system to perform a DDOS attack to any website he targeted. If you remember we discussed this in the starting of the book. Your computer acts as a slave for the hacker and participates actively in an attack targeted for a particular website.

4. **Spywares** as the name suggest are spy program which keep track of all your online activities and behavior. What websites you visit, what are your interests, what kind of deal you would be interested in, all this information is then sent to the hacker who can use it for malicious purposes.

5. **Adware** are the least dangerous of programs which get installed in your system along with

some genuine software as an add-on. These programs are intrusive in nature and display ads to you, redirect you to their advertising websites and installs unwanted software in your system. They are generally used by marketing companies to gain monetary benefit.

When your computer is infected by a virus, your computer needs antibodies to fight against it. Here, the **antivirus** software acts as antibodies and throws the virus away from the system. Unfortunately, many people are not aware of it and do not have an antivirus software on their computer at all. I would like to request everyone reading this to get an antivirus software for your computer if you do not have one. If you don't want to spend money on it, there are many free ones available which are more than sufficient for your daily needs. In fact, most companies offer a free unlimited version of the antivirus which will serve the purpose. If you ask my suggestion, I personally have used Avira, Avast, Quick Heal and found them good enough. Also please note that installing more than one antivirus won't increase your protection level but in fact slow your system down.

Ok, you have an antivirus on your system so you assume that no virus can enter your computer now. Well, things are not that easy. The way antivirus software works, it can only recognize already known classes of viruses, Trojans and key loggers. It cannot predict any future class of viruses (for correctness, I'd like to mention heuristic analysis by antivirus companies which attempts to predict future viruses, however for simplicity let's skip that). So basically if a hacker creates a new virus today, it won't be detected by antivirus software right away. It firsts infects some computer systems and then antivirus software analyze the virus to reach a conclusion that it is malicious. It is then added to the list of known viruses and anyone else infected by the same virus later on will alert the antivirus to remove it. For this very reason it is highly recommended to **keep your antivirus updated** all the time. Thousands of new viruses are created every day. If your antivirus is not updated, it won't find the virus from its existing list because the list is old. So remember to regularly update your antivirus. As a general rule, you should at minimum update your antivirus once a month (the more frequent the better).

How do malwares enter the computer?

Returning back to the biology class, there is very old saying that "prevention is better than cure". It is always better to prevent a disease from entering the body than curing it thereafter. Similarly, in computer world, it is always better to not allow a virus to enter the system rather than removing it after the damage has been done. There are two reasons for the same. Firstly, if you remove the virus after it has done its work, it might be possible that hacker has already compromised your account and changed your password so that you may not access it again. Also, the damage done to your files in the system might be irreversible. Secondly, if you are among the first ones to get hit by a new virus, antivirus software will not be able to protect you even if it is updated. So it is essential that you know how to stay away from the viruses and prevent them from getting near your computer. I am going to discuss the various ways people generally get infected by viruses:

1. **Downloading stuff from internet**

In this era of online revolution, one can find almost anything on internet. Be it music, videos, games, software etc. The problem is that we become so careless and impatient while searching that we literally click anywhere and download from any website to get what we want. This is certainly not a good habit. You should be extremely careful in where you download stuff from, because there are so many malicious files than you can imagine ready to be downloaded and infect your system. While downloading from torrent, always read the comments for any virus alert. Refrain from downloading cracked versions of paid software because most of the time they are infected with Trojans and it anyways is illegal to download them that way. If you like a software, consider buying it from the genuine website as it supports the developers who made it. If you cannot afford it, well nothing I can say but at least do yourself a favor by keeping away from Trojans. In case of other websites offering free software download of the paid ones, be extremely cautious and it is better to check the rating of the website itself. Same goes with the download of songs, videos etc. If you download something at least make sure you scan with an antivirus first to make sure it is safe for use. If an antivirus flag something as virus, DO NOT open the file under any circumstances.

 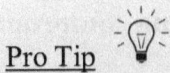
2. USB drives or external hard drives

Pen drives is another common source for spreading a virus. Hackers who creates such virus specifically write code such that it copies itself to any external drive connected to the infected system and when this USB drive is connected to a healthy system, the virus infects that one too and follows the same cycle. In fact one of the reason why computer viruses are called so is because their ability to imitate a real virus i.e. to make a copy of itself and spread. So, you have to be extra careful when you plug in a USB drive. Always scan the USB drive with an antivirus before opening it. When you are giving your USB to someone else, make sure to rescan it before opening it on your system.

3. Visiting compromised websites

This is another way of getting infected. What happens here is that a website may knowingly or unknowingly host virus on their pages which gets downloaded to the visitor's computer when the web page is opened. There are numerous variations to this attack, I'll explain the most common ones. Many times when you visit a website, it asks you to run a java component in order to provide you some service. For an example some website may offer you to download a video but to do so, it asks you give it the permission to run some component. You get a security prompt as below:

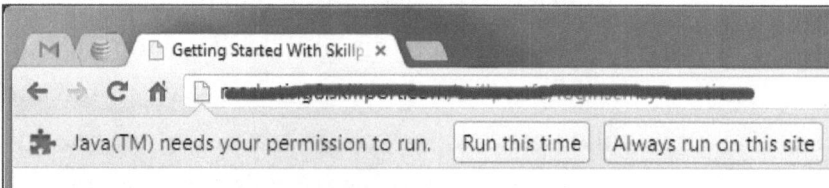

You may also get a dialog window shown as below:

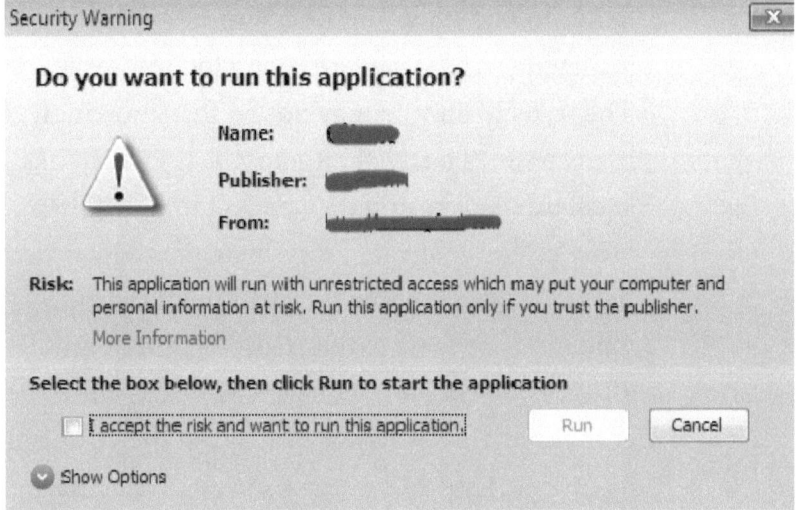

Most of the times, people just click on Run without even thinking about it. What you are basically doing here is allowing the website to download and run any file on your computer it wishes. So, if the website is trusted, you can assume it won't do you any harm. But about untrusted websites? There are thousands of such websites offering the user for something interesting and ask the user to allow their application to run and finally resulting in some virus or malware on the user's computer. For this reason, it is very important to allow only trusted websites to run such components on your system. If you are not sure whether to allow or not, it's better to not allow and find some alternate way of achieving what you were trying to.

The website may or may not do this knowingly, many a times hackers target websites which has substantial users and they hack it to inject their virus in the webpage. From then, the regular users of the website become prone to the infection. One more dangerous alternate version of this attack is where the user's permission to allow the component is not required at all, so the virus can be downloaded as soon as someone visits the infected website. Some people believe that it is not possible to infect someone just by clicking a link. Contrary to this belief, it is in fact very much possible. Using security vulnerabilities in the browser, it is possible for the attacker to download and run the virus on your system as soon as you click the link and the infected website opens in browser. For this reason, it is very important to keep your browser updated too. I recommend using Firefox and/or chrome browsers as they regularly update and patch the vulnerabilities. One more benefit using the chrome browser is that it protects you by tracking the website you are visiting and if and it maintains a list of all the websites which are harmful. If you try to access one of the websites from that list, you will be shown a warning page which is a good thing from a security perspective.

4. Email attachments

We all get lots of email nowadays. Email has become the prime mode of communication be it a formal or informal one. Hackers realized this very early and have always tried to use this medium to their advantage. One of the strategy employed by hackers is to attach the infected file with an email and send it as a mass email to people. Many people open the attachments and get infected with various kind of malwares.

If the attachments are dangerous, how do you know which attachment to open?

Considering the fact that any email can be forged (we discussed this earlier), i.e. we cannot be sure that the sender is actually the real one, you have to be extra careful.

Only open attachments from trusted sources and the ones you normally expect. For example if you get your phone and credit card bills on your email, you know it can be trusted. On the other hand, if you get a random email telling you to open an attached word file, do not open it. If you get an email from a friend who sent you an attachment, always cross verify with him whether he was really the one who sent it. In that case unless your friend himself wants to hack you, it is safe.

If you get a zipped file with an executable file inside it, you need to be extra careful. Those who do not know, every file has an extension at the end of its name in windows. For example the text files have an extension of **.txt**; audio files can have extension of **.mp3**, **.wav**; word file has an extension of **.doc / .docx** and so on. The first thing you should do is to enable the visibility of the extensions in folders. How exactly to do this is outside the scope of this book however you can find it easily on Google by typing "enable file extensions in windows 7/8/10"

After you have enabled the extensions view, be cautious whenever you get an **.exe** file from outside because it can potentially be a malware. Not all .exe files are malware though. Always ask the sender what exactly it does and scan it with an antivirus. Never in any condition open an .exe file from an unknown sender.

To further complicate things, even a word file can run a malicious .exe component inside it. On top of that, if the hacker is smart and uses advanced techniques, he can disguise a malware inside an innocent looking non .exe file. For example consider this scenario – you get an email from someone claiming a very funny video attached with the email. You download the attachment and it looks like below on your system:

Name	Date	Type
funnyvidexe.MP4	1/31/2015 9:44 AM	VLC media file (.m...

By the looks of it, no way it seems to be an executable file. It has extension of .MP4 which is used for videos, it has an icon of VLC media player. So the smart ones say, "No way can it be a virus or something. Let me enjoy the video." The file opens well and is in fact a funny video further confiding the user.

But what if I tell you that this file is fact a malware which installs a virus as soon as you open it. Sounds dangerous? It actually is. The attacker has disguised the extension and the icon to make it look like a harmless file. An actual funny video has also been bound to the virus which opens to gain the trust of user. So when you open this kind of file, a video will play but in the background the malware will be installed in your computer without your knowledge and you will never know what went wrong and when.

5. Installing software carelessly

Have you lost track of how many and what software have been installed in your system? Do you see unrecognized icons in your desktop? Do you feel that there is some mystical power controlling your computer because it behaves weirdly sometimes?

All these are symptoms of increased risk of malware infection in your computer and the result of careless software installation by you or another user of your computer.

Have you ever wondered why so many software we use are free cost? The developers of the software must have done some or a lot of effort in creating it so why they are giving it for free? Well, if you think that software developers are very generous and they do it out of moral duty towards the betterment of humanity then you are 99% wrong. While there are many genuine and trustworthy developers and organizations who do this but the people who have hidden motive behind giving free software are far more in number than the former. Even I am not doing a charity by writing this book. Although my intention is good, but I am also earning a profit from it; and by the way I will hunt you down if you have downloaded this for free ☺

Anyways the point is that a huge number of free software have adware bundled with them which gets installed along with the original software. Good news is that while installation, most of these software provide an option of not installing the additional adware. Bad news is that majority of people do not even care to read anything and just keep on clicking the "Next" button while installing a software. Developers know this and hence they take advantage of it by tricking the user into installing the additional crap. For example, let's see the installation of a free software called "Unlocker" which is a trustworthy and useful utility to unlock files in windows. When we try to install the unlocker software we are presented with the following screen:

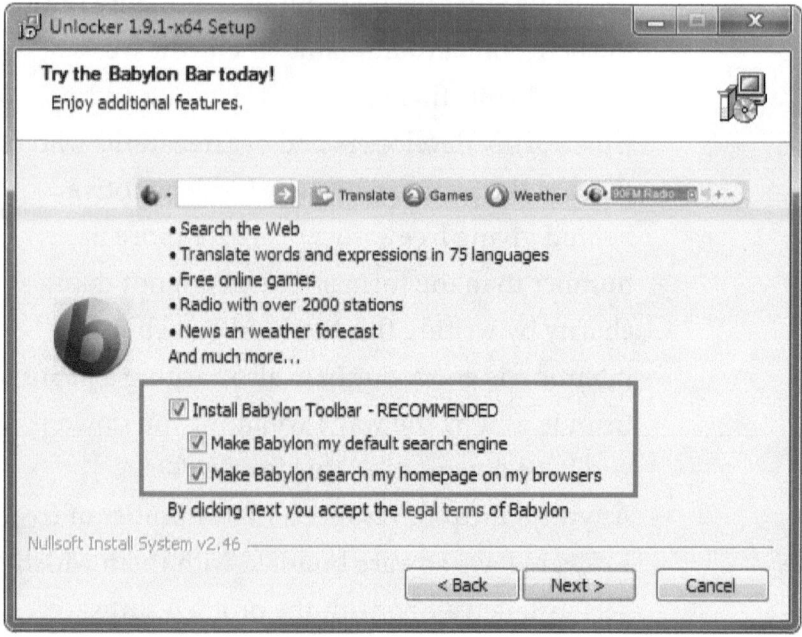

Notice that there is an option of installing something called as Babylon and the option is checked by default. This is a known adware which hijacks the browser. The unaware users just click on next without realizing that they are willingly giving way to some crap software into their system. The developers of unlocker utility earns money through this. That is why it is recommended to always read everything carefully while installing a software. Developing this habit will go a long way in keeping yourself protected.

6. Social networking

In a very short span of time, we have witnessed the rise of social networking websites like Facebook. Millions of people are being connected and are actively participating in this revolution. Unfortunately, this also means that hackers can now target a huge section of people at a single place. It's like a lion get to a farm of sheep and hunting becomes so much easy then. There are hundreds of malwares being circulated on Facebook every day. For example many of you might have seen your friends posting this kind link in their wall:

This is in fact a malware and when you click the link, it asks for your Facebook permission (so that it can spam the link to your friend's wall) and then installs a malware plugin to infect your browser. There are many similar crap which go viral on Facebook because of people not being aware of it. Some malwares are very annoying as they post and message on your behalf to all your friends and spam their space as well which results in humiliation for you.

Important things to keep aware of is to avoid these kind of stupid tricks. Always keep your eyes open and NEVER give permission to an untrustworthy application.

Sometimes we see posts in Facebook offering very interesting videos but when you click the link it redirects you to some other website. That website warns you that you need to install flash player to see the video and offers you to do the same within the same website. Remember, it is a trap when it does that. Genuine websites can only give a link to the real flash website of Adobe company. If a website is not doing that, then it is most probably installing a malware on your browser as soon as you try to install the plugin from within there.

So here is the tip – Never install plugins or browser extension from unknown sources. If you don't know what a browser extension is, don't worry; just remember not to allow any unknown application to install on your browser. You will always get a pop-up asking you to give permission to install it, if you are not sure what you are doing, do not give the permission.

When you are in doubt, ask some knowledgeable person about it. I have also provided a link to my Facebook fan page in the tips section. You can ask any question and I will certainly try to answer all your queries.

Let's now revisit our angel acronym –HACK and see whether it is able to secure us from these malwares. Using **A** for Antivirus update, more than half of the attacks by viruses and Trojans can be prevented. You should always make it a habit to regularly update your antivirus. Most antivirus have an option of auto update which you should enable if bandwidth is not a problem. Using **K** for Keep your eyes open, you can prevent the compromised websites from attacking you. Always check the links you are about to click and make sure you are not allowing any random website to run java or active-x components on your system. Also you should keep your eyes open while installing a software to prevent unnecessary components get free entry into your system. Using **C** for Common sense, do not open attachments from unknown sources and be aware with .exe files.

We saw that there are many ways your computer can get compromised via viruses, Trojans and key loggers. It is important to follow the safety measures discussed earlier to effectively guard against these kind of attacks.

To summarize:

Summary

✓ Viruses are dangerous programs intended for malicious activities
✓ Always keep your antivirus updates and perform an antivirus scan for external USB drives, downloaded programs, or anything you feel is suspicious.
✓ Keep an eye on websites you visit. Do not allow untrusted websites to run components if you are prompted with a security warning.
✓ Use secured browsers like Chrome/Firefox and update them regularly.
✓ Do not open attachments from untrusted sources
✓ Read carefully while installing any software on the computer.

Getting hacked – Wi-Fi sniffing

You went to a popular restaurant for dinner with a friend. The food is taking time to reach your table. You and your friend hang out so much that you have nothing much to talk and you both are just busy playing with your mobiles. Suddenly you realize that it is the last day for paying your electricity bill. The restaurant offers free Wi-Fi. What a good luck you have today, right? So you instantly paid your electricity bill online using the restaurant's free Wi-Fi and thereafter checked in your Facebook status – having dinner with my best friend at ***. Oh wait, the food has also come and it looks tasty as hell. What a fine night you are having. So the two of you enjoy every bit of slice and discuss how easy life has become after the advent of technology and after everything has become available online these days.

The next morning, you wake up from the bed and check your phone for missed whatsapp messages when suddenly you see this text:

*"$10,000 has been successfully transferred from your bank account ****** to the account xxxxxxxx. Available balance: $12.45"*

You are instantly shocked to see this. All your savings from past year just vanished in thin year. You decide to call the police but they suggest you should rather contact the cybercrime department. After a long struggle of six months, you give up the chase. Apparently the hacker was very smart and cops are not able to snatch him or at least it appears so.

What went wrong here? This can really happen to any of us. It is the human tendency to take things for granted which never happened to him/her. But really if we work so hard to earn money, why not be a little careful to protect it. That is the least we could do. To explain what exactly happened in this scenario and how to prevent it from happening, let us understand how it all works.

Wi-Fi has become a very common technology used by millions of people to access the internet. However potential loopholes in the underlying technology has left a lot of room for the hackers to attack and exploit the wireless networks. Please note that securing a Wi-Fi setup is a topic on its own and I am not going to cover it here since it requires some technical skills and is outside the scope of this book. Still in one liner I would like to comment to those people who have set-up a Wi-Fi network (not the users), to follow some basic guidelines, like using WPA and WPA2, not using

WEP, not broadcasting the name of the network etc.

For a normal user who just uses a Wi-Fi connection to gain access to internet, here is a fact: everything you do over a Wi-Fi network is completely unsecure if you are not taking special measures to secure it. Basically, any user who is connected to the same Wi-Fi network as yours can sniff your data and use it for his advantage. For that reason, I have only single advice for this section – **DO NOT** use public Wi-Fi network to access your email or confidential data like banking etc. Because you do not know who all are connected to the same network. Since it is open and free, an attacker can connect to the same network and monitor all your activities. Without going into technical details, let me warn you that all your passwords are also prone to attack and can be easily hacked by the attacker. If you are like me who understands things better with a diagram, here it how it works:

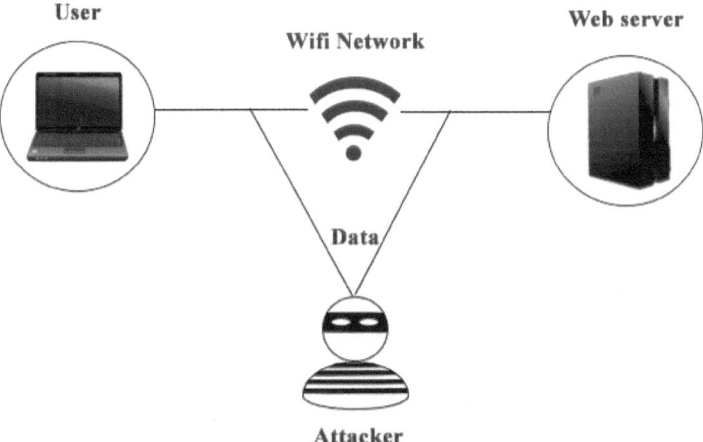

As you can see, before your data reaches the server, an attacker sniffs in between and copies all the data to his computer which he can later manipulate in different ways like grabbing passwords and other sensitive information from it. So, follow this thumb of rule – NEVER use public Wi-Fi for sensitive work. You can browse the internet in general but try not to login to your online accounts. That's it for this chapter.

Getting hacked – Social Engineering

Social Engineering is a technically hyped word for online scam and fraud. It's like some educated technical person stealing your money instead of a regular roadside thief. Whatever you call them, it has become the most enticing way for the fraudsters to earn quick money. Just one time effort of building up a technical way to set-up a trap and they enjoy the fruits for a long term. Ok, enough of promoting the crap, did I tell you that those who are caught end up doing a major portion of their life in jail.

Social engineering means manipulating people into doing something which results in monetary benefit to the attacker either directly or directly. There are literally so many variations of this attack that it is impossible to cover all. However I will give examples of a few and leave it your C for Common sense to smell foul from a distance.

The Banker

John has an account in the Elite bank which holds all of his lifelong savings. John works as a sales manager in a top firm. One day he gets a call which changes his life. Let's read the conversation:

Caller: *"Hello, May I speak to Mr. John Walker?"*

John: "*Yes, speaking.*"

Caller: "*Sir, this is Marie from Elite bank. Can I have a moment of your time please? It's regarding a new policy update which we want you to be aware of.*"

John: "*Ok, tell me.*"

Caller: "*Due to some regulatory changes, we are decreasing the interest rates on the savings account. So, from now on it would be 2.5% instead of the previous 4%. This would take effect from next month. Also, I can see that you are a loyal customer of Elite bank for a long time. We are launching a new product for the old customers offering attractive return on investments.*"

John: "*Sorry, but I am not interested.*"

Caller: "*Sir, I request you to hear me out. If you don't like it, you can opt out. This product is aimed to retain our loyal customers and the bank is keeping only a low margin passing on the huge profits to customers.*"

John: "*Alright, humor me.*"

Caller: "*Thank you, Sir. In this new investment scheme, bank will invest the customer's and its own money in an automated software trading application. The software is extremely smart and automatically captures the anomaly in stock market. It then automatically do the trade resulting in high profits. The software's owner company needs a client to prove their product and hence are offering a risk free trial. The bank is passing on the benefit to its customers.*"

John: "*What about the authenticity of the software company? What if they default and fail to offer risk free return?*"

Caller: "*Good question. The software company is among the top 10 ranking in world, due to security reasons, I cannot disclose the company's name. Regarding the failure of that company, bank is offering full protection to its customers. In the unlikely event that it happens, bank would bear the loss and will return the customer's money with the standard 2.5% interest rate. It's a win-win situation for the customer. That's why we have limited the number of participating customers to just 100, so that bank's losses are also minimized.*"

John: "*What is the expected rate of return with this investment?*"

Caller: "*The software company claims a return of 20% per annum but our analyst reached out at a figure of around 16%. This is expected rate of return which may be higher or lower. The bank however guarantees a minimum of 6% return in case the software company doesn't default. If it defaults, as I told you earlier it would be 2.5%*"

John: "*Alright, I am interested. How do I get in?*"

Caller: "*Thank you, Sir. As a first step I would like to ask how much money you would like to invest. Minimum of $100 is required and maximum is $100,000*"

John: "I'd like to play safe. $1000 is fine for now".

Caller: "*Alright Sir, I will need to debit this amount from your account. You will get a text message and an email with all the relevant details as soon as the amount is debited. To debit the amount, I will need your internet banking details like username and password. I will do the transaction from here.*"

John: "*Ok, my username is johnwalker85 and password is Reliant@512*"

Caller: "*Thank you Sir for the details. Within 10 minutes you will get the confirmation. All the very best. Any more question for me?*"

John: "*No thanks. I'll call if I have any issues*".

Caller: "*Alright, have a good day Sir. Bye*".

A few minutes later, John receives a text informing him that $245,000 has been debited from his account. He is taken aback. At first he thinks it might be a mistake by the banker who he authorized to invest $1000 from his account. So he calls the bank, informs the customer care about the incident and finds a shocking truth that bank never called him at the first place. Hearing this, John almost passes out. His feet feels like so weak that it is impossible to stand. He has been saving this money for so long and all of a sudden it is all gone. He never even dreamt of this. It took a while for him to realize that he has been a victim of online fraud.

What went wrong?

The call pretending from the bank was quite convincing as initially it started with only informational content aiming at gaining the trust of victim. However John should never have decided instantly for the investment but instead he should have asked the official brochure/web-link or any other supporting documents regarding the new product. However the point where John lost all his money was when he gave his online banking credentials to the caller. You must have heard this before but NEVER provide your net-banking details to anybody. Any employee of the bank would never ask for it and even he does you should never give it. Because that's what happened in this case. The scammer used John's credentials to wire money to his accounts. Needless to say, John should have used **C (HACK)** for common sense.

The generous donator

Ben is a Physics teacher in a school. He received the following e-mail:

Hello my friend,

Hope this day finds you well?, I am Ony Obo a merchant in Nigeria, I have been diagnosed with Esophageal cancer, It has defiled all forms of medical treatment, and right now I have only about a few months to live, according to medical experts.

I have not particularly lived my life so well, as I never really cared for anyone (not even myself) but my business. Though I am very rich, I was never generous, I was always hostile to people and only focused on my business as that was the only thing I cared for. But now I regret all this as I now know that there is more to life than just wanting to have or make all the money in the world.

Now that God is about to call me, I have willed and given most of my property and assets to my immediate and extended family members as well as a few close friends. I want God to be merciful to me and accept my soul. I have decided to give also to charity organizations, as I want this to be one of the last good deeds I do on earth. So far, I have distributed money to some charity organizations in the U.A.E, Algeria, Sudan, Europe and Kenya. Now that my health has deteriorated so badly, I cannot do this myself anymore.

I once asked members of my family to close one of my accounts and distribute the money which I have there to charity organization in Bulgaria and Pakistan, they refused and kept the money to themselves. Hence, I do not trust them anymore, as they seem not to be contended with what I have left for them. I will want you to help me collect my last deposit and dispatched it to charity organizations which I deposited in security/finance house abroad, which no one knows of is the huge cash deposit of (Twelve Million Eight Hundred Thousand U.S dollars) I have set aside 25% for you, then 5% for any expenses incurred.

If you are interested, please send your prompt reply to my private email address below which you will have to reply to if you will be kind enough to assist;
Email: bigiXXX@yahoo.co.uk
God bless you
Ony Obo

I hope many of you already know that this is a scam. Those who really believe this e-mail and that some unknown Nigerian merchant is going to transfer millions of dollars to your account, well my friend, this world is not so nice. What this seemingly harmless and riskless deal sounds would later turn in the scammer asking you to pay thousands of dollars as fees for various fake legal documents and processing fees etc.

You will be amazed at how many people actually end up paying those amounts and get scammed. People who actually fall for this kind of trap are either too gullible or too stupid or both. Remember, there are good deals and there are too good to be true deals. If something sounds like the latter, it most probably is.

In general, to identify these kind of traps, you need to ask the following questions:

- Does somebody want to transfer millions of dollars into your account?
- Does someone want to pay you to cash cheques and send them the money?
- Met a new friend on a friendship/dating site who's asking you for money?
- Has a dying person contacted you wanting your help to give his money to charity?
- Have you sold an item and are asked to accept a payment larger than the item amount?

If the answer to any of the above is 'Yes', then it is a SCAM. Don't fall for traps like these. Fight them and spread awareness among your friends and family.

E-whoring

One common social engineering technique is called as e-whoring where the scammer poses as a hot girl and chats with desperate men online. Remember the old days of chat rooms? There still are many and the scammers find those desperate men very easily in social networking sites, chat rooms, and xxx websites. To make it look convincing, scammer posts multiple fake pictures of some girl but the most convincing trick they play is when they actually allows the victim to see the girl live through a web-cam. There are many software available which manipulates a picture to make it look like it is connected live with webcam. So when the victim ask the fake girl to stand up, scammer just a click a button to play the animation of girl being standing up. It looks very much real.
When the victim is convinced, the scammer asks for money either directly or through gifts like Amazon gift card, gift vouchers etc. The scammer may also ask to click some links, complete surveys which result in monetary benefit to the scammer.

One variation of this kind if scam is using bots or automated programs instead of actual scammer being online. This is less convincing but you will be surprised to know how many people fall for even this kind of nonsense.

One guy even posted online that he made $279/day by just e-whoring people.

Work from home scam

How many of you have seen online ads like the below:

This is certainly not the only one offering such insanely high income by working online. There are hundreds of such fake schemes ranging from 'work from home mom' to 'mystery shopping' scams. These scammers try to make it very enticing for the user to join their fake program and they play every kind of dirty trick to convince the victim. For example the offer may be coming from a news-like website. The user thinks that this being coming from a news channel should be legitimate when in reality the website would be fake. The comments section is also faked many times to fool people into believing that other people actually have tried the scheme and are happy with it. These websites will track your location and then display you the fake testimonials of people near your region so that you are tricked into believing that it is true. The way these fake schemes make money is by asking the user to pay an upfront joining fee or by selling the user their cheap product at high price. In fact you can identify such schemes that way. If it offers you to earn substantial amount of money by doing some petty job but then asks you pay some fees upfront, it is SCAM. Don't fall for it. Certainly, there are some legitimate business where you can earn some extra cash, but the number of scams exceed the legitimate ones by a huge margin. To identify the scam just use your common sense and ask yourself – why would the company give me such amount of money for doing this? Or why is it asking me for money upfront?

Below is the list of common lines thrown at the user to entice him -

"Work at home Mom Earns $6,795/month"

"Discover how this Work from Home Mom has earned a Living during these tough economic times."

"Interesting, statistics show that in 2012 internet employment rates have nearly doubled compared to last years. I found myself a new job"

There are far more types of online scams that you can imagine. If I were to list all of them, it would be a book in itself. Important thing is to use common sense and not fall into these traps.

General Tips

Now that we have discussed all the possible ways where you can be at risk, let me also provide the readers with some general tips which if followed correctly will go a long way to get you from trouble. These tips complement our existing knowledge and along with the acronym – HACK, will guard you against most of the digital threats. So let's get to it right away:

Tip # 1: Enable two factor authentication
Most email and other service providers offer two factor authentication nowadays. Those who do not know what that is, two factor authentication provides an additional layer of security which requires the user to do a secondary authentication (generally through phone verification) in order to get access to the service. Gmail users might get constant reminders to enable it if not already done. I highly recommend to enable this on all important websites you care about as it prevents the hacker from logging in even if he somehow gets your password. If the website does not offer two factor authentication, you cannot do much about it but if it does, please enable it.

Tip # 2: Use strong password

You might have noticed that in none of the previous sections about the ways of getting hacked, have I used the letter **H** for - Hard password as a recommendation from the acronym **HACK**. The reason is very simple, it is the most common suggested tip by everyone when in reality it is least useful one and least hindering block for an attacker. We have already seen in previous sections that you can have the strongest of passwords but can still be hacked very easily. However this doesn't mean that you should not have a strong password. There are scenarios where it is very much necessary:

1. If an attacks hacks the database of a website where you have an account, he has to crack (decrypt/solve in simple terms) the password to view it as text, otherwise it is in garbage form. The probability of hacker being able to do it is directly dependent on the complexity of your password. So if you have a very simple password, it will take only minutes to crack it whereas for a complex password it might take years (for which most hackers don't have the time and resources).

2. Even if the website is not hacked the attacker might try to login (using automated tools) by guessing the credentials using all the combinations of letters and numbers. If you have a simple password, it would take very less time for the hacker to find it.

3. There are a few other scenarios too technical to discuss here where having a strong password is a necessity.

If you don't understand the above points, don't worry. Just remember to have strong password and you'll be fine.

One thing I would like to point out here is that just by using incorporating numbers and symbols, a password doesn't become strong. It is important that you do not use common guessable words in the password. So if your name is Rakesh Gupta and you use Rakesh@Gupta22 as your password, this is not at all strong. Similarly, your birthdates, telephone numbers, month and place names etc. are a strict No. While deciding for your password, just ask yourself a question – How easy it is for your best friend or relative to guess the words in your password (not the whole password, even parts of it)? If the answer is that it is quite easy, I suggest you think of another password.

Tip # 3: Do not use a single password for everything

You should never share passwords among the websites. Most of us have the tendency of using a common password for all the websites as it is simpler this way and we don't have to remember different passwords for different websites. However this is not at all a wise thing to do. I personally learned this lesson the hard way many years back when I got to know that a website (my account was also there) was hacked and all the user's information was made public. I was very disappointed and scared to see my password being posted like a notice board. The fact that I used the same password for all my accounts made it more dangerous and I immediately changed password on other websites. Thankfully no harm was done to me but this is not always the case with other people. If remembering different variation of password seems a challenging task, you can use various password manager software which are available for free on internet; so you don't need to remember the passwords for individual websites. I personally use '**Last Pass**' software which works fine for me, is available for all common browsers and is free.

Do not save your password in the browser because it is very easy to fetch all those passwords and if your system gets infected by a malware, all the passwords may be sent to the attacker. That's why it is important to use a dedicated password manager software rather than just saving in the browser.

Also instead of having absolutely different passwords on different websites and later on regretting why you bothered to go online, what you can do is to have different passwords for different category of websites:

Casual websites: You can use a simple password because you don't even care if your account gets compromised here. Probably you won't visit the website again but had to mandatorily create an account. You can save the password in the browser if you want apart from the password manager.

Regular websites: Facebook, Gmail etc. where you visit on a regular basis. You should use fairly strong password and if possible use different variations for different sites. You should not save these passwords in the browser, however you can save to the password manager.

Important websites: Your internet banking websites, office accounts, monetary related websites which are very important to you. Use extremely strong passwords and remember them by heart. DO NOT save these passwords to password manager and don't even think of saving them in browser.

Tip # 4: Install WOT plugin

WOT is a free plugin available for all major browsers which is extremely useful while surfing online. WOT stands for **Web Of Trust** and is very true to its name. It shows you the rating of every website you visit and whether it is safe or not. Here is how it looks:

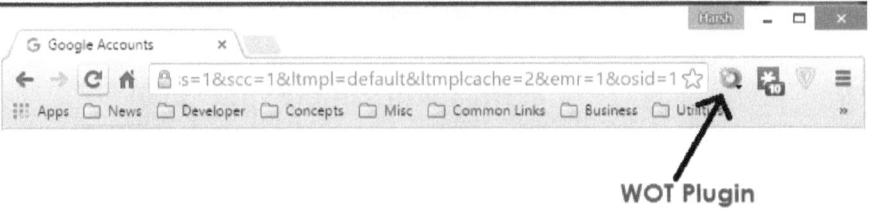

WOT Plugin

The little circle is green when the website is safe to visit (Gmail in this case) and it changes its color to orange/red for unsafe websites. Just a quick glance at the plugin while visiting an unknown website instantly tells you about its reputation and whether or not it is safe to proceed. You can also see the details and people's comment for the website which is very useful. This plugin is one of my highly recommended tool for everyone.

Tip # 5: Install Malware bytes

Malware bytes is an anti-malware software which works similar to the anti-virus. If you remember I told you that you should not install two antivirus on the same machine. However an anti-malware is different and is supposed to compliment the antivirus. There are some kinds of malware which remain undetected by the normal anti-virus software but an anti-malware like Malware bytes detects that. It is perfectly safe to install Malware bytes alongside an antivirus. It only compliments it and adds an extra layer of protection.

Tip # 6: Do not distribute your email

Let's face it. We are asked to provide our email id at so many places while surfing online and we do not think twice before even doing so. Although there is no harm as such in distributing your email, problem arises when you freely submit your email in every website you visit and soon your inbox becomes so cluttered that it becomes a challenge to find out important mails among the plethora of useless junk. Also, the more places you submit your email id to, more are the chances of you getting scam emails. Although after reading this book I am sure you can identify such messages, it is better if we don't get to test ourselves in this area. So, try not to distribute your email like you are doing charity, try to limit its audience.

One thing you can do is to create a separate email id specifically for browsing purposes and keep your official or regular email only for important updates or communication. This way even if you get scam emails in the other id, you won't get confused.

Pro Tip

You can distribute your email after modifying it for the specific use case. For example if your email id is harsh@gmail.com, and you visit a dating website, then submitting harsh+dating@gmail.com will also send the mails to your inbox, however now by looking at the 'To' field, you can identify the reason for the additional spam emails.

Tip # 7: Be careful at cyber cafe

Many times either due to emergencies or because of other reasons we end up in a cyber café to get our work done. However sometimes this can be a reason for your account getting compromised. The computers at the cyber café are open for all public so they are prone to intentional all kind of attacks including key-logging, shoulder surfing camera recording etc. The trap may be set-up by one of the café's customer or even the café owner himself. The computer might contain malwares which track every information about your activities including your passwords. So it is best avoided to use a cyber café for online transactions. If it is unavoidable, at least use a virtual keyboard to minimize the risk. Also, one way to be absolutely sure that the café-owner is trying to scam people is by looking for what is called a hardware key-logger. A hard-ware key logger is similar to its software counterpart with a basic difference that a hardware key logger is not invisible unlike the software one. A hardware key logger is generally attached to the CPU of the computer and looks like this:

Notice the key logger device being plugged in between the CPU and keyboard wire. So the next time you see anything like this in a cyber-café it is better to run away, or better still inform other customers about the café-owner's doing.

Tip # 8: Scan suspicious files online

The antivirus software installed in your computer might do a good job if you keep it updated.

However, when you are suspicious of a particular file being sent to you, it is a good idea to scan the file using online antivirus services. There are websites (like www.virustotal.com) which can scan any given file through multiple antivirus software which decreases the risk of you being infected particularly if the threat is new in market. For example virustotal.com currently runs the uploaded file through 55 different antivirus software compared to just one installed in your computer. It doesn't takes much time and gives you a sigh of relief whenever you are in a confusion regarding a file.

Tip # 9: Always ask whenever in doubt

This last tip is certainly not the least. There is no shame is asking when we don't about something. Especially when it is a matter of security we can never be too careful. Whenever you are in doubt about something which you think is a security risk to you, find people around who you think are knowledgeable and ask them about your situation. If immediate response is not necessary, you can also drop me a question on my Facebook fan-page named "Maurya's anti hacking tips" and I will try to answer your query as soon as I can (Ok yes this was a marketing trick).

Quiz Time

Although you can skip this section but I suggest you not because after giving the test, you will get to know how much you have actually learned from this book. You will be given 20 questions in the form of MCQ (Multiple Choice Questions). Each question carry 1 mark and there is no negative marking for wrong answer. After the test is over, you can compare your results with the below chart which will gauge your awareness level:

Score	Awareness Level
0	**Zero.** No person on this earth is qualified enough to teach you anything. Please apply for a refund.
1-5	**Uninformed.** You probably have not read the book at all and just skipped to test section.
6-10	**Novice.** You need to learn a lot of things. Please go through the book again or stop using internet.
11-15	**Attentive.** You were not sleeping in class which is good. There is still room for improvement though.
16-19	**Informed.** You are now officially a member of the geeks club who know everything.
20	**Nerd.** Just one word, respect.

The answers to the question has been provided at the end. Some questions are tricky intended to test your common sense. Please do not cheat and best of luck.

Q 1 – Which of the following is not a motivating factor for a hacker to carry out an attack?

a) Monetary benefit
b) Sending out a message
c) Personal grievance
d) All of the above are a motivating factor

Q 2 – You received an email from bank saying that some information update is required because of a new regulation. How would you update the bank information?

a) Update using the link provided in the email.
b) They will call if it is urgent, so don't bother to do anything since it might be a trap.
c) The email is fake and you should not respond to it.
d) Try updating through the official bank's website.

Q 3 – A friend of yours sent you a funny game to play. It seems very interesting but you are not sure whether to open it. What should you do?

a) The sender is your best friend. He will never harm you, so you should not worry and just play the game.

b) Since the game is an executable file, you should not open it.
c) Confirm from the friend about the game but run it through antivirus before opening.
d) Ask your friend whether he actually sent it and if he says yes, there is no need of scanning through the antivirus.

Q 4 – Which of the following cannot be a source of malware infection?

a) Social networking websites.
b) Installer of a trusted software company.
c) A friend's USB drive.
d) All of the above can be a source of malware.

Q 5 – You are in a market when your Mom calls you and reminds you to pay the water bill immediately? How will you pay the bill?

a) Use the public Wi-Fi connection available in market.
b) Use the public Wi-Fi connection but use a secured connection.
c) Wait till you to reach home.
d) Drive 30 km to submit the bill manually.

Q 6 – You get a call from your insurance company about a new scheme. However you need to decide immediately since the offer is only for a few customers and they are asking to transfer $10,000 to an account to secure your offer.

   a) This is possibly a fraud call. You should report it to the authorities.
   b) Convince them to secure it for a lesser amount like $1000.
   c) Just transfer the amount. It does not looks suspicious.
   d) Transfer the risk to your friend and ask him to pay on your behalf.

Q 7 –You meet a new friend on Facebook. She seems trustworthy and request you to send her a little gift from Amazon. What do you do?

   a) The gift is not expensive and she looks cute. Just buy her that gift.
   b) Try to settle her for a cheaper gift.
   c) Just transfer the amount. It does not looks suspicious.
   d) Do not buy her anything and stay cautious from then.

Q 8– You found a website that pays $10,000/day for doing very little work?

a) Run away from the website and never come back again.
b) Seems interesting. What's wrong in trying it out?
c) Sign up only if they don't ask for any money.
d) Call the police emergency number for possible fraud.

Q 9– You are at a cyber café and notice an unusual device at the back of CPU?

a) It might be some sort of advanced technology.
b) Pull it out and throw it away to the dustbin.
c) Do not use that cyber café again.
d) Punch the owner on his face for trying to hack you.

Q 10– Which of the following is a strong password?

a) StrongPassword
b) !December@12
c) 12345678
d) Bal42gal

Q 11– Where should you store your passwords?

a) On a paper insider your wallet so that no one has access to it
b) Save it on the browser
c) Use a password manager software
d) Save it on an email and send it to yourself.

Q 12– Which of the following cannot be a source of malware infection?

a) Microsoft Windows CD.
b) An image file.
c) File downloaded from the internet.
d) Email attachment.

Q 13 –You meet a new friend on a dating site. She has been talking to you for a long time now and she ask you to meet somewhere?

a) It is not safe. Meet her at a public place only.
b) Since it is a dating website, it is safe to meet her.
c) Take the cops along with you as a security measure.
d) Tell her that you don't want to meet her and never contact her again.

Q 14- A friend of yours offers you a method to earn some extra cash. You have to sign-up and refer 50 friend of yours for it to get activated. What will you do?

a) Your friend is a smart guy. You trust him and do what he says.
b) This seems fishy as company is asking for 50 referrals before even starting.
c) This is a standard procedure nowadays so no worries.
d) Call the cops to arrest your friend.

Q 15– Which of the following is a weak password?

a) ILoveSuperman
b) !<3RedGuy
c) Crazy4Sum1
d) %CryptoN%PlAn3T

Q 16 – There is a viral video circulating on Facebook, everyone seems to be sharing it. You are also interested in seeing it but the website tells you that flash player is missing from the browser.

a) The website allows to install it directly. No need of going somewhere else.
b) Try installing from the official website

c) Try with a different browser and if it fails only then install it directly from the video website
d) Uninstall the browser from computer and try again

Q 17 – You opened a website for downloading a software however there is a warning by Google that the website might be unsafe to visit. What should be your next steps?

a) You absolutely need the software so you anyways go ahead and download it
b) Do not open the website
c) Scan the webpage with an antivirus
d) Surrender yourself to the cops for downloading software illegally

Q 18 – You received an email about a lottery you won amounting to $100,000. Your husband/wife was not aware of these scams so he/she replied to them and gave them your personal details. You deny them to pay the fees they asked for but now they are calling you and threatening you with life. What should you do in this situation?

a) Stop receiving their calls and block their email.

b) Pay them the money they are asking for to get rid of the situation.

c) Immediately write to the cybercrime department telling them everything about the incident

d) Call the cops

Q 19 – Which of the following tip is not relevant in regard to staying safe from phishing attacks?

a) Use strong password
b) Install WOT plugin
c) Keep your antivirus updated
d) Do not distribute your email

Q 20 – Which of the following internet habits can lead to your account being compromised?

a) Keeping the antivirus updated
b) Always checking the URL of websites you visit
c) Blindly clicking links you encounter while surfing
d) Regularly changing the password of your accounts

_____End of Test_____

Answer key

1. **D)** All the factors are valid for any attacker to carry out and attack

2. **D)** Since the e-mail could also be from the real bank, you should visit the official bank website to check.

3. **C)** Confirming from the friend is necessary and so is scanning it through an antivirus.

4. **D)** All of the options can be a source of malware infection including the installers of trusted companies as they may incorporate adware to generate revenue.

5. **C)** Even a secured connection is not safe in a public Wi-Fi set-up.

6. **A)** You should be able to identify such calls.

7. **D)** You are most probably a victim of e-whoring

8. **A)** Probably Bill Gates uses that website to get rich. It is not for us.

9. **C)** You seriously didn't think of hitting the guy, right?

10. **D)** Although it does not contains special characters but it is still better than the rest. December is a month name which constitutes a weak password.

11. **C)** It is the safest among the given options. Although the best one would be to store it all in your brain forever.

12. **A)** An original CD of Windows would definitely be malware free since you already paid so much to get it.

13. **A)** If you selected D) why did you even start dating in the first place?

14. **B)** Although arresting your friend would be the next best option.

15. **A)** which contains the name of famous personality

16. **B)** You should always install stuff from the official sources.

17. **B)** Option D) is also correct if you really mean it

18. **D)** Really you should be calling the cops here. By the time cyber-crime department would read your message you would probably be dead (one way or the other).

19. **A)** Using a strong password does not help when you are a target of phishing.

20. **C)** Do I really need to explain this one?

Final Words

I really hope that this book helped you in understanding the atrocities of todays' online world and that now you may be more aware and proactive in dealing with such situations. I'd love to hear your feedback and comments. You can either do it at the place where you got this book from or you can write me at contact@harshmaurya.in.

With that said I thank you for your time, hope to hear from you. Stay Safe!!

References

Image credits:

http://nsfocusblog.com/2012/10/29/ddos-attack-and-defense/
https://commons.wikimedia.org/wiki/File:Phishing.JPG
https://en.wikipedia.org/wiki/File:Keylogger-hardware-PS2-example-connected.jpg
https://pixabay.com

General information:
http://www.getcybersafe.gc.ca/
http://wikipedia.org

www.ingramcontent.com/pod-product-compliance
Lightning Source LLC
Chambersburg PA
CBHW022113170526
45157CB00004B/1616